I Promise You A Rose Garden

For sometime I have been wanting to share some of the things that have helped to give me more confidence in painting roses. I DO promise you a rose garden if you will practice and take one step at a time until you gain more and more control and understanding. Ideas for designing as well as structural and color helps can be found in the following pages. Happy Painting!

Mary Jo Leisure

COPYRIGHT © 1982, Mary Jo Leisure. Enjoy painting for fun and/or profit. Designs and instruction may be used for teaching. Mechanical reproductions prohibited without written permission from Mary Jo Leisure.

I Promise You A Rose Garden

Let's begin by going over the structure step by step. The rose below is completed. Notice the structure beginning on page 3.

5.

Begin your projects small and then gradually build more involved designs. I particularly like roses and fruits designed and painted together. Designed above is a red rose and red cherries on a black background. A simple design but yet it can be very effective depending what you paint it on. Use your imgination.

Red Roses
STEP BY STEP

The roses in this book begin with a fluffing in of the color. In transferring your pattern you only need the outside line to show the form before applying your paint.

1. In fluffing in the color use the full flat brush thinking fluffy — cloudy — or airy. Work with your background. Some part of your painting should nearly be the same value as your background. The colors used here are:
   Fluff/ GL + BK — GL + CRL — CRL.

2. Back petals are painted first. Don't clean your brush out with turp — just dry wipe and then continue to load lighter colors on top outside edge of your brush. You do not have to concentrate on double loading when you have a fluffed in background.
   Overstrokes/ Various mixtures of
   CRL + GL — CRL + YO — Or + NYL + (W)

3. & 4. Begin the bowl by painting the inside petal first and then working yourself to the outside, **sometimes** connecting the rows. You must have a good sharp chisel on your brush in order to get nice fine edges. Always apply more pressure on the top outside edge of the brush. This helps to keep control and have good clean lines.

5. Outside, open petals are last. Think of the petals as wrapping around each other. Begin with more pressure creating a larger stroke (such as a comma stroke) and then come up on the chisel and get skinny as you come toward the middle of the rose. You can come back and place added darks as well as sparkles of light to create a better shape.

Colors for the leaves and cherries as well as the pattern can be found on page 13.

Palette Loading Instructions

Liquitex Oils
Cad. Yel. Lt. . . . . CYL
Cad. Orange . . . . Or
Cad. Red Lt. . . . . CRL
Barn Red . . . . BR
Prussian Blue : . . . . PB
Dioxizine Purple . . . . Diox. P.
Ivory Black . . . . BK
Raw Sienna . . . . RS
Bt. Umber . . . . BtU
Naples Yellow . . . . NY

Rembrandt Oils
Naples Yellow Lt. Ex. . . . . NYL
Titanium White . . . . W
Yellow Ochre . . . . YO

Grumbacher Oils
Thalo Yellow Green . . . . . TYG
Geranium Lake . . . . GL

1. Run your brush through paint on your palette numerous times before using it. It takes more paint on your brush than with other subjects. The rose is a combination of stroke and blending and it is important that your brush is loaded well.

2. Your brush needs to have a good sharp chisel. Either a sable or composition brush works well. Preferably the bristles are not too long.

3. When applying your paint be firm with your pressure on the outside edge. The inside edge of your brush will lift slightly helping to blend the fluff into your color.

4. It takes three types of strokes to build your structure.
    a. Petals across the back of the bowl.
    b. Petals in front of bowl.
    c. Outside bottom petals.

The colors are brush mixed. The + sign means pick the colors up together on your brush. The — sign means dry wipe your brush and then pick up the next color. The ( ) sign means maybe or a small amount. Leave room around the paints on your palette to load your brush well and test your color.

a.    b.    c.

Pink Roses

STEP BY STEP

Background Rose Petals VTH Acrylic

1. Fluff in color using choppy pressure strokes in a circular motion. (refer to page 3)
   Colors used to Fluff/ GL + RS — CRL + YO — NY

2. Overstrokes — Back petals first. Make the strokes irregular enough that you cannot count them without thinking about them.
   Overstrokes/ CRL + CYL + NYL — Mix + W + (CYL)

3. & 4. Close in the bowl beginning with the inside petals first. Lift brush then apply again to create the effect of more petals.

5. Complete rose by adding outside petals next. Refine — deepen and hilite. Burnish some edges with GL + RS.

See pattern on page 49

Leaves

#1 Dk/ Bk + CYL + (W)   #2 Dk/ GL + RS
   Lt/ Mix + CYL + W   Lt/ TYG
   S/ Mix + Bk   S/ GL + RS + BK
   Hi/ Mix + W   Hi/ Mix + TYG + W
   (W creates a cool look with mixture)

1.

2.

3.

4.

5.

Painting

1. This little design has two roses, five leaves and a few squiggles. Think through what your painting order will be before you begin.

2. I paint top objects first, therefore I painted the rose that was on top of everything to begin with. Fluff the rose in with GL + RS — CRL + YO — NY. Overstroke with mixture + CYL + W — W (Or).

3. The next object under the rose just painted is the second rose. Apply fluff first where you feel the most obvious dark is. Be firm as you apply the paint so you have control of the clean up. The fluff in this rose should be a little deeper such as GL + BtU.

Order

4. Overstroke accordingly. As you get to where the two roses meet work carefully. Don't press too hard as you want this area to be darker and look as if it is complete.

5. Paint the leaves in order as well, doing top leaves first. Look for two values in the dark area. This will break the outline and create more shape. Stems and linework are done last.

Porcelain Bell

The porcelain bell was a delight to paint. I added Italian composition gold leaf on the band and edges. This gives a touch of elegance. The bell makes a lovely decorative accessory.

Porcelain Bell

After applying the pattern to the bell, I rubbed a little color in the background. I applied it with a brush using linseed oil plus RS + Bk and then rubbed it out in a circular motion using a kleenex.

Roses
Fluff/ CRL + RS — OR + YO
Overstrokes/ CRL + YO + NYL + (CYL)
  Mix + W + (CRL)
Burnish/ GL + RS

(Underneath rose has more white and is a lighter value)

Leaves
Dk/ BK + CYL + (W)
Lt/ Mix + CYL + W
S/ Mix + Bk — Mix + GL
Hi/ Mix + CYL + W — W

Strawberries
Dk/ CRL + RS
Buff/ CRL + YO
Lt/ Mix + NYL + (CYL)
S/ GL + RS
Hi/ W + (CYL)
Seed and texture

Lighter berry is basecoated with NYL. Add shading and hilite. Thin paint with turp to apply linework (Green Mix, Hi/ Mix + W)

Roses and Green Grapes

Roses
1. White
Fluff/   BK + RS — YO + RS — YO
Overstroke/   Mixtures of W + YO + (CYL) — (NYL)
S/   Bk + (RS)
T/   CYL

2. Yellow
Fluff/   GL + RS — RS + BK — YO — NY
Overstroke/   NY + YO + NYL
                NYL — NY + (CYL) + (W)
Burnish/   CRL + RS
S/   BK

Leaves
Dk/   Coxgr + Bk
Buff/ YO
Lt/   Mix + NY + (CYL) + (W)
S/   Mix + Bk
Hi/   Mix + (CYL) + (W)
T/   Bk + W — CRL + RS

Grapes
B/   YO + TYG
S/   Mix + Bk
Hi/ TYG + (CYL) + W — W
T/   CRL + RS — OR

Dk/ Bk + YO (Coxgr.)
Lt/   YO + TYG
S/   Mix + Bk
Hi/ Mix + TYG + W — W
T/   CRL + RS — Or

See project in color on page 35

Background — Black acrylic on masonite
Spray with Krylon Matte Finish before applying pattern.

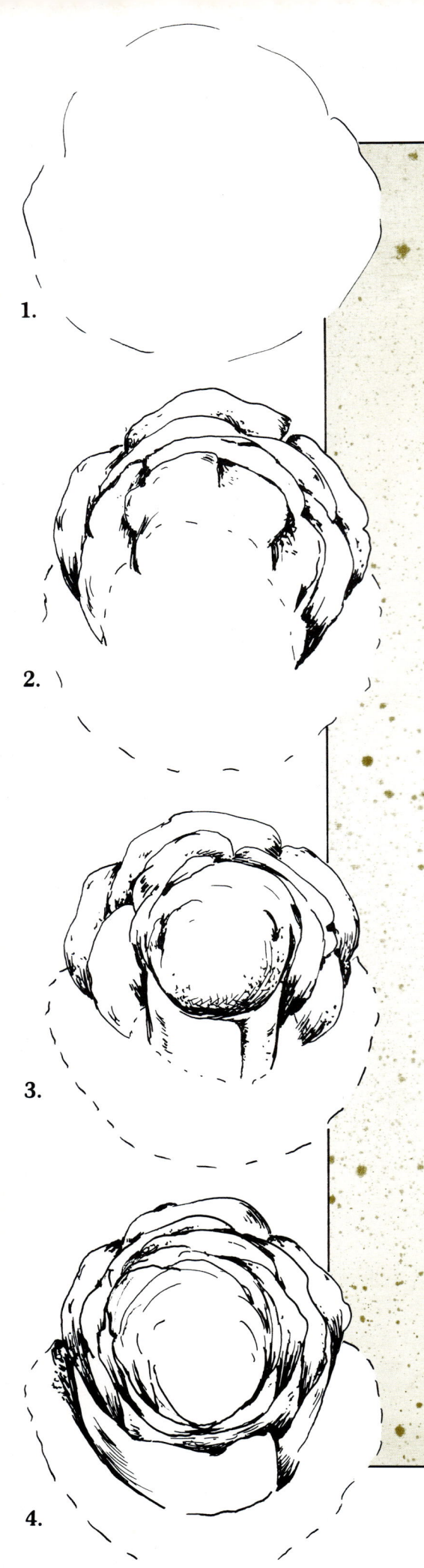

1.
2.
3.
4.

Helpful Tips on Structure

1. When fluffing in color work for three values. Use your brush flat with curving pressure strokes similar to shape of flower. Leave some background showing. Keep paint very dry.

2. Work back row of petals first finishing with tightness of bud. Try not to row the petals up too evenly. Don't clean brush with turp, just dry wipe. Load top edge (about 1/3 of brush) with light mixtures. When applying color apply more pressure to top outside edge of brush.

3. Close in bowl beginning on inside petal first. Connect some rows — not necessarily all rows. Lift brush and begin again to create more petals.

4. When applying loose outside petals work back and forth from right to left twining petals. Look at full rose on page 13. Burnishing edges, applying tints, adding second value darks and strengthening sparkle (hilites) bring life to your rose.

To practice use a dry brush (without paint) to stroke over pattern helping you to develop pressures to achieve shape.

This is the pattern for the design on page 2. The following is color set up for leaves and cherries on a black background. Color set up for rose is on page 3.

Leaves
Dk/ PB + OR
Buff/ YO
Lt/ Mix + (NY) + (CYL) + W
S/ Mix + Bk + (PB)
Hi/ Mix + (CYL) + W
T/ OR
Accent/ GL + (BK) — GL + CRL

Cherries
Dk/ GL + BK
Buff/ GL + CRL — CRL + YO
Lt/ CRL + YO + NYL
S/ GL + BK
Hi/ Or + NYL — NYL + (CYL) + W — W
T/ OR — BK + W

See in color on page 2

See in color on pages 17-18-19

Patterns for other sections on pages 16 and 17

Roses
Fluff/ GL + BK — GL + CRL — CRL + YO
Overstroke/ CRL + GL — Mix + NYL + (CRL) + (OR) + (CYL)
S/ GL + BK
T/ BK + W — CRL + GL

Leaves
Dk/ BK + CYL
Buff/ YO — RS
Lt/ Mix + CYL + W
S/ Mix + BK + (PB)
Hi/ Mix + CYL + W — W
T/ OR + YO + (CRL) — BK + W

Angel
Facial Features
 Flesh/ YO + CRL + W
 Base face leaving features open
 Shade with deeper flesh tones
 Hi/ Flesh + W — W
 Detail eyes, nose and mouth
Hair
 B/ RS
 S/ Bt U
 Hi/ NY + NYL

How about painting a sleigh? It could be used in a little antique bedroom stuffed with pillows or maybe a plant. At Christmas you could fill it with gifts accenting the holiday season. The background on the sleigh creates a lot of breaking areas. I stained a section with Bt. Umber and painted a section with Pearl Touch VTH acrylic. I accented a large area including inside, with Black acrylic, and then trimmed the edges with Avocado Green and a true red acrylic. Refer to overall pictures on page 17.

This little porcelain box was trimmed with gold leaf and decorated with a white rose. Use color set up as shown on page 47.

Roses can really decorate anything, even this graceful porcelain seal. Pattern on page 22.

20

Apricot Beauty

This goose is an "Apricot Beauty." With its graceful lines it could be placed anywhere.

The graceful wooden goose has been decorated with roses across its back. It could be used as a bookend, doorstop or just to add that splash of color. Pattern and instructions on page 24.

Everything's Coming up Roses

PATTERN FOR SEAL

Tied with pink roses around the neck of this porcelain seal. I touched the eyes with green from the leaves.

Roses
Fluff/   CRL + RS — YO — NYL
Overstrokes/ Mix + NYL + W + (CRL)
S/   GL + RS

Leaves
Dk/ BK + CYL
L/   Mix + (CYL) + W
S/   Mix + BK + (PB) + (GL)
Hi/ Mix + (CYL)
     + W — W

Ribbon
Dk/   RS + BK
Buff/ CRL + YO
Lt/   NYL
S/   Mix + BK
Hi/   W + (CYL) — W

Everything's Coming up Roses

The porcelain penguin is delightful. I gold leafed his stomach and his eyes. The rest was left in sharp contrast using pen and ink on the white to create the design.

Apricot

ROSES:
Fluff/ CRL + RS — YO
   GL + RS + (CRL) — YO — NY
Overstroke/ CRL + YO + NYL + (W) + (CYL)
Deepen/ RS + GL + (BK) — Diox. P. + RS
Burnish SOME edges to show up
on light background.

Background: Pearl Touch, VTH acrylic and trimmed with Apricot VTH acrylic. After pattern is applied rub some color around pattern using a mixture of CRL + YO + NYL + W with your oil paint using linseed oil as a medium. Apply with a brush and rub out with a kleenex in a circular motion. Fleck with green mixture + YO using turp as your medium.

Vary the values of the roses by either adding more white and NYL or more dark such as GL + RS. Remember, adding yellow to your mixture helps to keep your pink color soft.

LEAVES:
Dk/ BK + CYL
Buff/ YO
Lt/ Mix + (CYL
S/ Mix + Bk
   Mix + GL
Hi/ Mix + (CYL
Lighter value leav
light value gre
accordingly.

BRANCH:
B/ RS
S/ GL + RS
Hi/ Mix + TY

Linework is thinne
Use middle valu

Beauty

Neck Pattern

This is another way to display the lovely porcelain ornaments. The ball is made with cornhusks and trimmed with lace. A touch of mistletoe could also be added. Planning your painting into your holiday decorating can add that something extra. Each year I add a little more painting.

See page 29 for ornament patterns.

Wreath

This tiny grapevine wreath was sprayed with antique white and trimmed with ribbon, baby breath, and tiny porcelain bells painted with roses. Take a small rose pattern, place it on the outside edge cutting off part of the pattern. This could be used in a wall grouping for that touch of something different.

Ornaments

Here are a few patterns that may be used on the porcelain ornaments shown in this book. You can either pen and ink and tint them or paint them. Use the colors of your choice using the color set-ups and the step by step sections in this book.

Rose patterns are easy to design. Place the roses back to back or use a single rose and frame with leaves. If the painting surface of the ornament is an awkward shape place the design from an outside edge.

"Rose Petals"
See in color on page 44

"Ring Around Of Roses"
See in color on page 34

Ceramic Pitcher
See in color on page 35

Room Full of Roses

I would describe this as a dressy primitive. The slatted wood creating the primitive effect and the painted delicate roses creating the dressy effect. This is a twin bed where the roses fit the cutout trim of the headboard. The desk is a very old piece which has been painted to match the beds. Gold leaf on the trim and porcelain drawer pulls add a touch of elegance. Outside edge of bed is gold leafed as well.

Room Full

This shows the outline of the top of the headboard. The pattern is on pages 50-55. One color set up is given on the roses and the leaves. Concentrate on the value change as you are painting.

ROSES
Fluff/   GL + RS — CRL + RS — YO — NY
Overstroke/   Mixtures + W + (CYL) + (CRL) + (OR) — W
S/   GL + RS + (BK)

# of Roses

LEAVES
Dk/   BK + CYL + (W)
Buff/   YO
Lt/   Mix + (CYL) + W + (TYG)
S/   Mix + BK
Hi/   Mix + (CYL) + (W) — W
T/   TYG — BK + W — Or
Basecoat very light value leaves.

BRANCH
B/   RS
S/   RS + BK
Hi/   TYG + W
Add linework and flecking to add a more finished look.

Ring Around of Roses

This porcelain piece was designed by gluing two round plates together. The back and edges of each plate were gold leafed. The ring of roses on the large plate was pen and ink and the design on the smaller one was painted. Use colors of your choice. Pattern on page 30.

These plates came from the porcelain collection of Zim's in Salt Lake City, Ut.

The ceramic pitcher is one from Ceram-Tole in Joplin, Missouri. I painted the ceramic pitcher a black acrylic and trimmed it with gold leaf.

Pattern and Instructions on page 10. For Roses and Grapes — Pitcher page 30.

Roses for Santa

This cutout Santa head was pen and inked over a stained background. This projects a primitive or nostalgia look. The roses were painted with metallic gold and the holly was painted in greens. The Santa could be used as a door decoration, centerpiece or get brave and do something different. Add handles and make a serving tray out of it.

Ornaments

Again another way to display the porcelain ornaments. These ornaments were pen and inked and then Bt. Umber was rubbed behind the pattern. The ornaments were also trimmed with golf leaf.

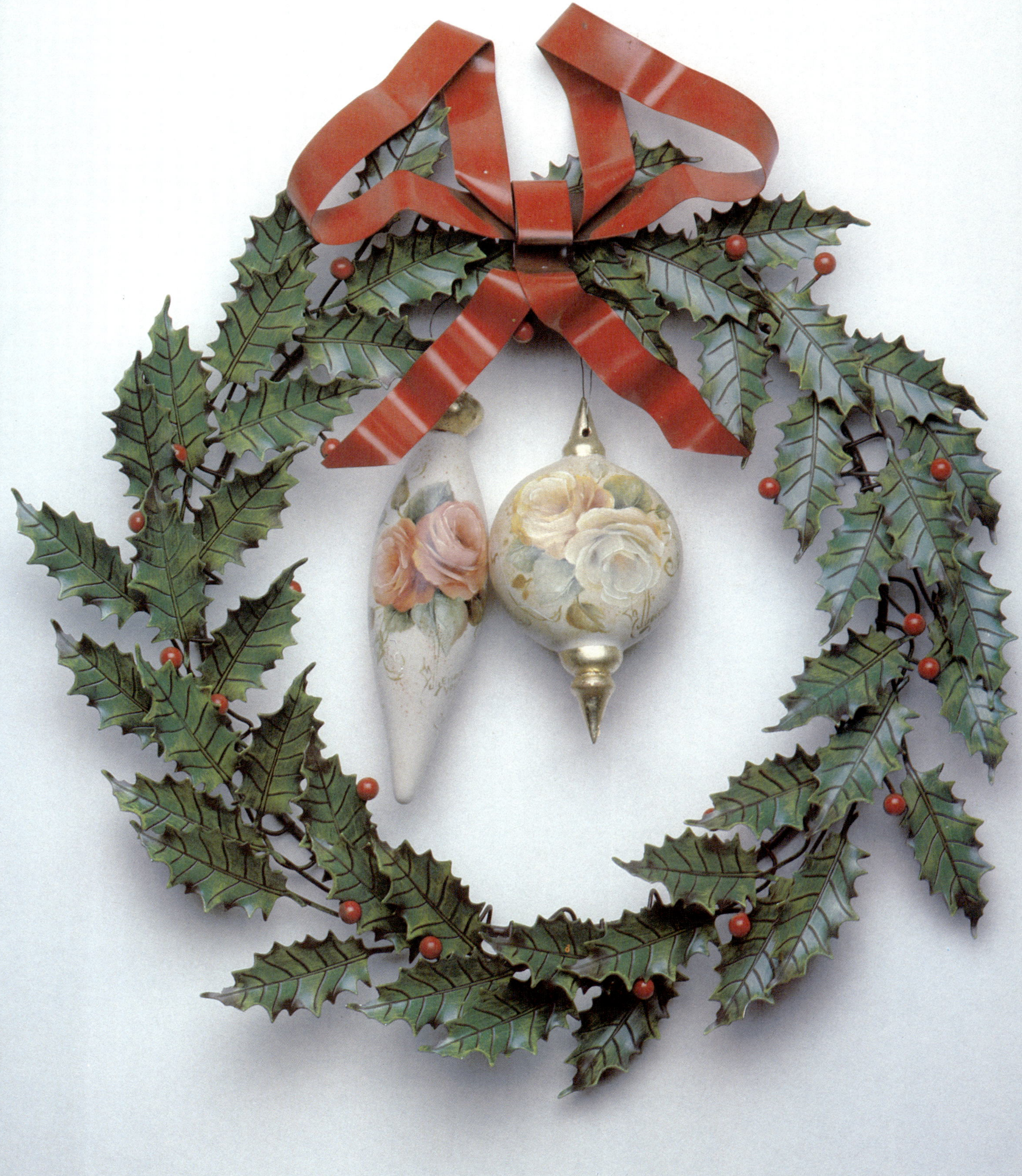

Fairy Lamp

Use colors from the Pink Rose on page 5

The Fairy Lamp has excellent painting area. A portion was gold leafed for elegance.

A Glow of Roses

Porcelain frames these salmon colored roses. They seem to glow when the candlelight touches them. This little box was fired a soft green that has a cool cast. I trimmed it with gold leaf.

SALMON ROSES
(Keep two values by varying the lights and darks)

Fluff/   RS + GL — RS + CRL — NY
Overstroke/   RS + CRL + NY + (NYL) + (W) + (CYL)
S/   RS + GL + BK

For white rose and leaves use color set up on page 47.

Hearts and

These dimensional hearts were decorated with roses and trimmed with lace and ribbon. They could be used as tree ornaments, package ties, a special touch added to a wedding or just a decorative accessory in that little antique bedroom. The hearts are available from the Village Tole House in Arlington, Tx. See address on page 64.

More Hearts

These hearts come red in color and in three sizes. I sprayed some of them with Krylon Antique White. Use the color set up in other areas of this book to get the color of your choice.

Rose Petals

The dried rose petals spilling from the little round cheese box accents this single painted rose. The top of the box was painted Pearl Touch and the sides were painted Apricot. Both are Village Tole House acrylics.
Pattern in on page 30.

Covered with Roses

This oval porcelain box was designed with the painting flowing from the lid to the bottom of the box. The color set up is the same as white roses on pages 46 and 47.

Pattern on page 26

5.

White Roses

STEP BY STEP

This white rose was painted on London Fog, a Village Tole House acrylic. It is a mid value background.

1. Fluff/ RS + BK — RS + BR — RS + YO
   Balance the colors with fluffing in of color.

2. Overstroke/ Back petals first and then working several other rows. W + NY or (YO) + NYL + W + (CYL)

3. Close in bud as tight as you wish. Don't start color too light. With that dark fluff be sure to add plenty of yellows.

4. As you continue to close in the bowl continue to add lighter colors. A touch of CYL with your White helps to keep your white clean.

5. Add outside petals at bottom wrapping your petals around one another. Refine by adding additional second value darks, burnishing and tinting. Work it into your background in some areas.

Pattern and instructions for the single rose with leaves and berries on page 48.

White Roses

See Step By Step on Pages 46-47

LEAVES
1. Dk/   BK + CYL + (W)
   Buff/ YO
   Lt/   Mix + CYL + W + (TYG)
   S/   Mix + Bk
   HI/   Mix + (CYL) + W
   T/   Or — CRL + RS — TYG

   Hi/   Mix + (CYL) + W

2. B/   RS + (BR)
   S/   RS + BK
   Hi/   Or + NYL — W

BERRIES
   B/   Or + (NYL)
   S/   CRL + (GL) + RS + (BK)
   Hi/   Or + NYL + (CYL) + W — W

Pink Roses

PINK ROSE
Use color set up for rose on page 5

Yellow Roses

YELLOW ROSE
   Fill in Flowers
   Soupy with turp/ RS + GL —
                      CRL + RS + YO
Dk to Lt/   NYL + CYL + W

   If you get these too intense use
a cool tint to soften (BK + W)

LEAVES
Dk/ BK + CYL + W
Lt/   Mix + CYL + W
S/   Mix + BK + (PB)
Hi/ Mix + (CYL) + (W) — W
T/   RS + CRL — BK + W — TYG

Headboard

*Dotted line shows outside edge of bed.
Pattern is on pages 50-55*

Pattern in full
Use as guide to help
put pattern together.

Left edge of headboard

52

Right edge of headboard

53

Top middle to right edge of headboard

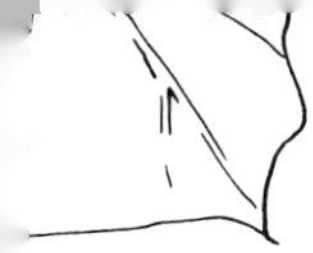

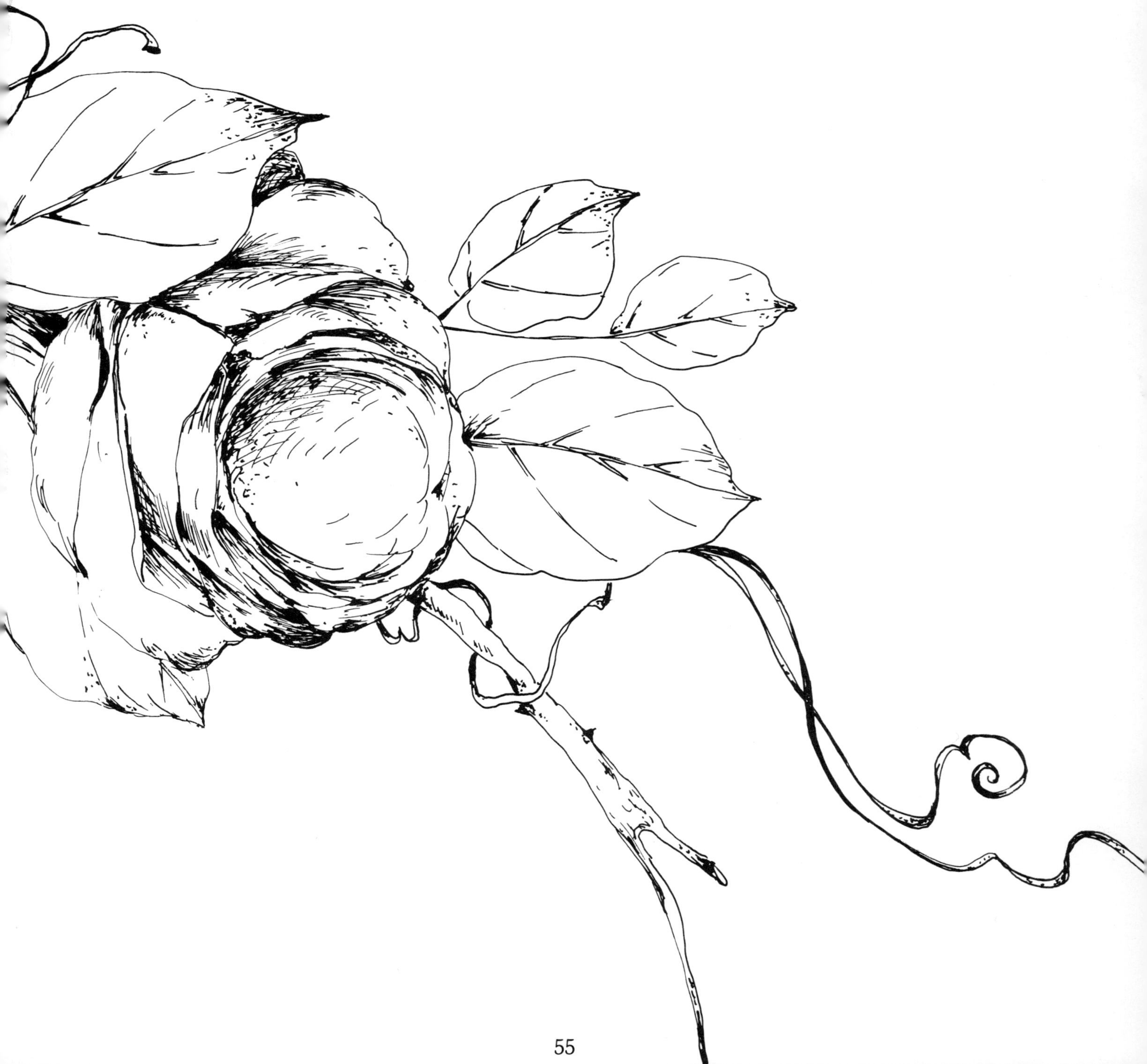

Tied with Roses

Porcelain Egg Box

ROSES
Vary rose values
Fluff/   GL + BtU — GL + RS — CRL
               + YO — NY
Overstroke/   GL + RS + NY — NYL — CRL
               + YO + NYL + (CYL) + (W)
               GL + BtU

RIBBON
B/   NYL + YO
S/   GL + BtU
Hi/   W + (CYL)

LEAVES
1. Dk/   BK + CYL
Buff/   RS
Lt/   Mix + CYL + W
S/   Mix + BK
Hi/   Mix + CYL + W — W
T/   BK + W — CRL + YO

2. Dk/   RS + GK
Lt/   TYG
S/   RS + GL + BK
Hi/   Mix + TYG + W

This porcelain egg box was fired a soft dusty pink. I rubbed deeper rose tones behind the design using GL + BtU

Porcelain egg box with a touch of the past.
The mirrored black piece hanging on the wall is a very old piece given to me by my youngest daughter Lynnae. Notice the painted stroke roses.

Roses in Gold

Roses In Gold show metallic gold roses painted on a large wooden plate which is stained with BtU and painted with black acrylic. The back and edges are trimmed with gold leaf and the stained edge is bordered with black and BtU stroke work. The metallic gold oils were used on the overstroked light edge. The fluffing in was done with BtU — RS and deepened with BK. Leaves were done with the same colors.

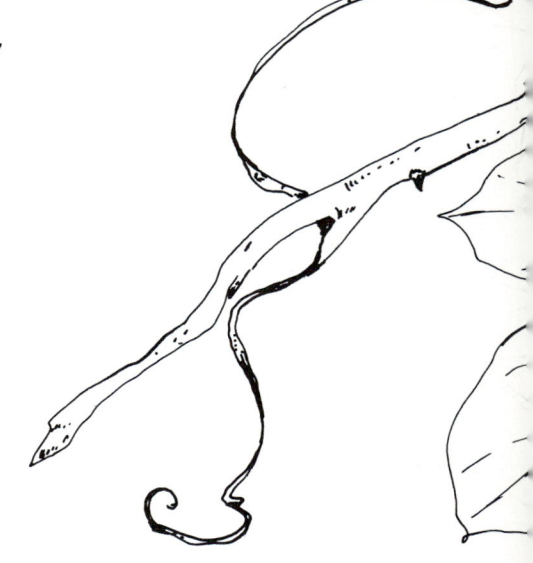

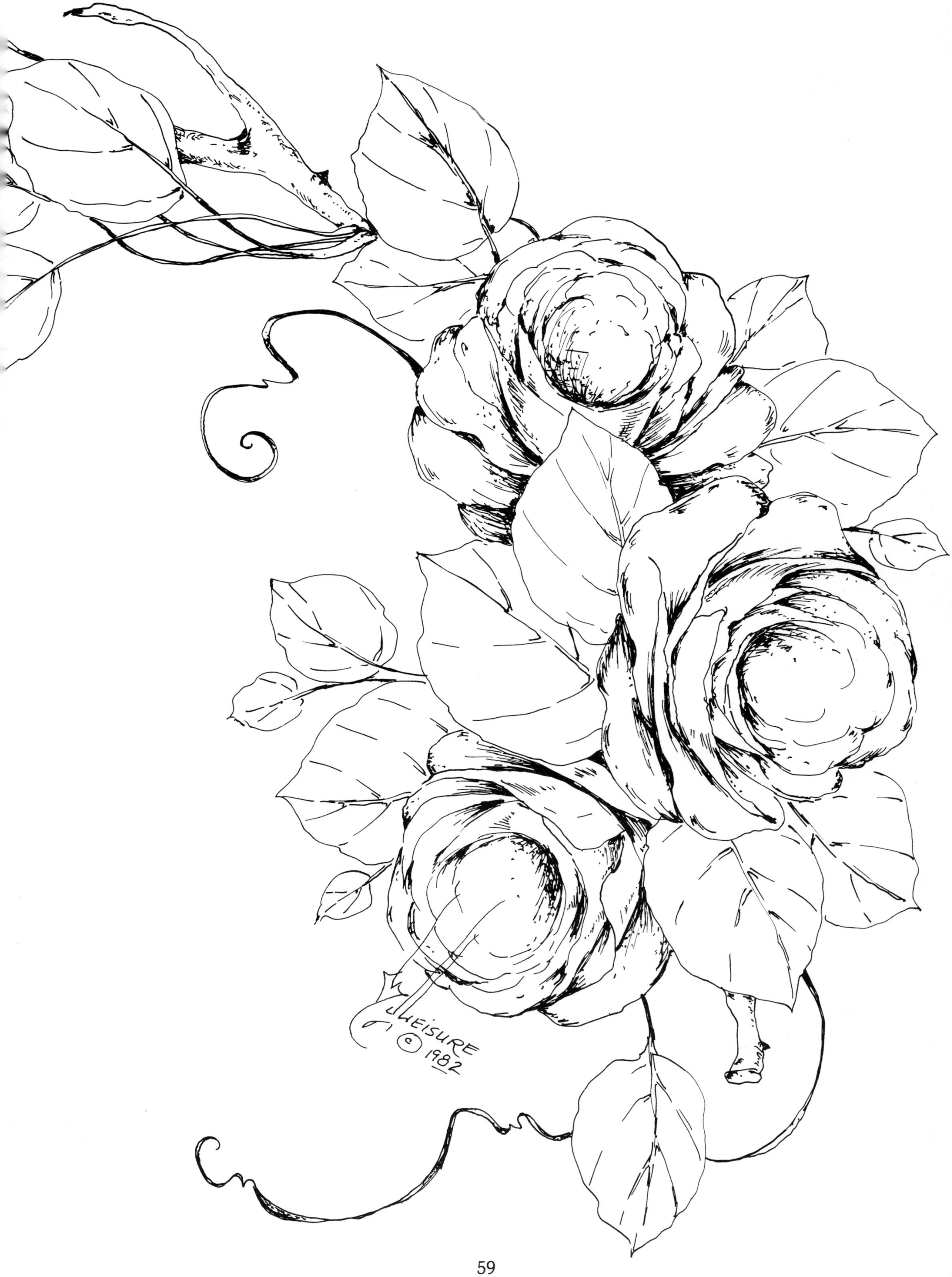
LEISURE
© 1982

Roses and Berries

Background Black acrylic trimmed with gold leaf.

ROSES
Fluff/   GL + BK + (Diox. P.) — CRL
                 GL + BR + RS — YO + Or + CRL
Overstrokes/ Mix + NYL + (CRL) + (Or) — CRL + GL
                 YO + Or + W + (CRL)
T/   Accent/ CRL — Or

LEAVES
Dk/ PB + Or
Buff/ RS — YO — Or
Lt/ Mix + CYL + W — W
S/ Mix + BK + (PB) + (GL)
T/ TYG — Or — CRL

BERRIES
B/ Mixtures of BK + PB + Diox. P. + GL
Hi/ W
Sparkle/ W

See project in color on front cover

Porcelain Heart Box

Trimmed with Lace

This heart shaped porcelain box was trimmed with lace. It makes a lovely gift for any occasion. Use color set up from page 11.

62

Yellow Roses
STEP BY STEP

1. Fluff/ RS + BK — RS + CRL — YO

2. Overstroke/ Beginning with back petals using mixtures of YO + CYL — CYL + W + + (NY) — W — NYL

3. Begin bowl working from the inside to the outside. Use deeper overstroke mixture to begin with (YO + CYL)

4. Complete bowl ending with lighter overstroke mixtures.

5. Finalize rose completing bottom outside loose petals. Tint with Or + NYL. Deepen and hilight accordingly.

Pattern and additional color instruction on page 49.

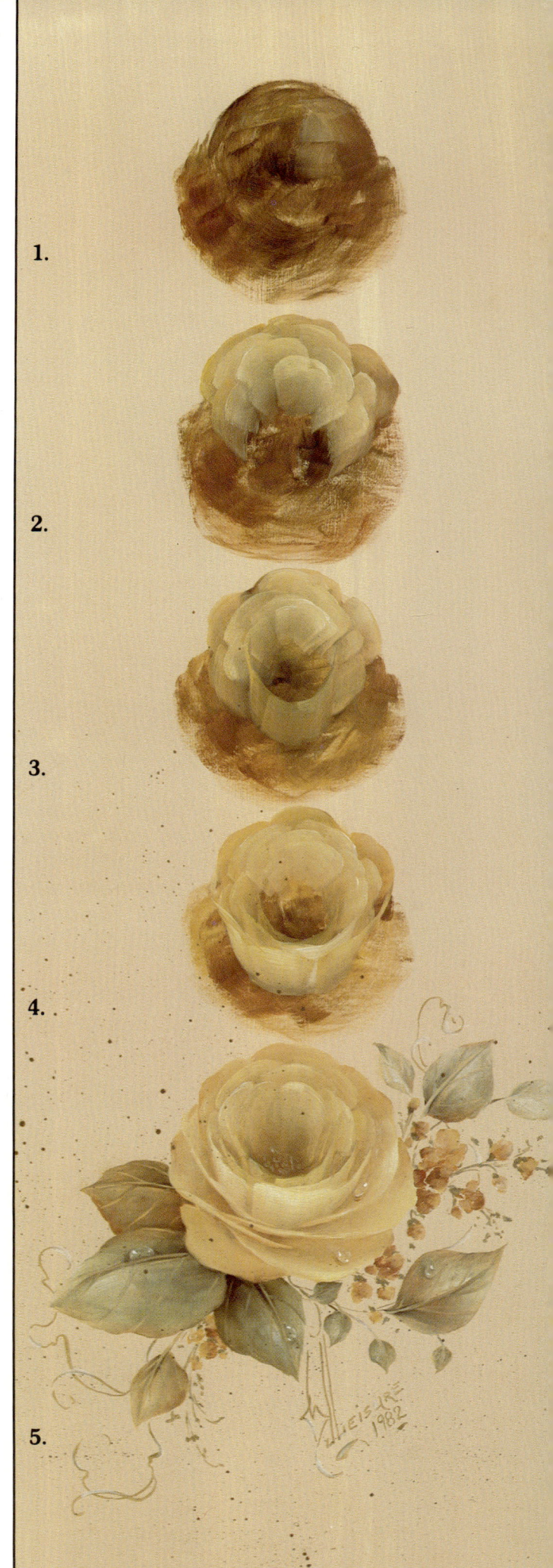

63

I hope your rose garden grows and becomes lovelier the more you paint. Don't be afraid to experiment. Use different colors. Design to fit your needs. Keep your painting interesting with variety.

The porcelain pieces I painted on were made by Ada Belle Davis unless I mentioned differently by the project. To add a touch of something extra I added gold leaf to a portion of each porcelain piece. The pieces are beautifully made and a delight to paint on. They can be poured in several colors. For catalog send $1.50 to Decorative Porcelain Ltd., 1515 Evergreen Pl., Tacoma, WA 98466.

If you are unable to find some of the backgrounds which I have painted on in your area send your request to Village Tole House, 314 N. Pecan Arlington, TX. 76010.

May I encourage you to become a member of the National Society of Tole and Decorative Painters, Inc. if you are not already one. The Society will keep you in touch with the decorative painting world today. Write: NSTDP, P. O. Box 808, Newton, Ks. 67114.

Happy Painting

PUBLISHED BY:	PRINTED BY:	PHOTOGRAPHY BY:
Mary Jo Leisure	Trafton & Autry Printers	Wyatt McSpadden
3917 Gatewood	P. O. Box 9068	P. O. Box 1673
Amarillo, Tx. 79109	Amarillo, Tx. 79105	Amarillo, Texas 79105